Your Amazing Itty Bitty™ Guide to the Pro Cheerleading World

15 Simple Secrets of Triple Threat Pro Cheerleaders Based on Firsthand Experience

Haley Marie McClain Hill

Published by Itty Bitty™ Publishing
A subsidiary of S & P Productions, Inc.

Copyright © 2024 Haley Marie McClain Hill

All rights reserved. No part of this book may be reproduced or transmitted in any form or by any means, electronic or mechanical, including photocopying, recording, or by any information storage and retrieval system, without written permission of the publisher, except for the inclusion of brief quotations in a review.

Printed in the United States of America

Itty Bitty Publishing
311 Main Street, Suite D
El Segundo, CA 90245
(310) 640-8885

ISBN: 978-1-959964-92-6

Have You Ever Wondered What it Takes to Become a Professional Cheerleader?

Here are your 15 firsthand secrets to achieving that dream.

In the dazzling world of professional cheerleading, putting on the iconic uniform and stepping out onto the field is nothing short of a dream come true.

In her book, Your Amazing Itty Bitty™ Guide to the Pro Cheerleading World, Haley Marie McClain Hill acts as your coach, teammate, and mentor and provides you with guidance to achieve your goal. Not only will you uncover the inside secrets to the pro cheerleading world, but also gain essential principles applicable to any profession. From how to prepare for tryouts to stepping out onto the field for your first game, you'll be highlighting every sentence in this book.

You will discover:

- The art of pro cheerleading tryouts
- Effective communication strategies
- How to navigate team and coach dynamics
- Proven techniques to nail your newfound stardom
- And so much more!

If you're eager to explore the thrilling world of pro cheerleading from the inside out, this essential Itty Bitty™ book is for you!

I dedicate this book to my mom, Tracy Sloan. Thank you for doing everything in your power to make sure I was cared for and successful in my life. I wouldn't be the woman I am today without your love and dedication. I am forever grateful and love you so much!

Also, thank you to my Penn State cheerleading head coach, Curtis White. You have made a tremendous impact on my life, from giving me the opportunity to even be on your team to traveling to games and tournaments around the U.S. You are family and I cherish our memories together!

And to every cheerleader I have ever cheered with: thank you for pushing me past my limits, holding me accountable as a teammate, and becoming some of my very best friends.

Finally, I dedicate this book to you, the reader! Your inner drive and love of cheer and dance has brought you here and I couldn't be more proud of you for prioritizing your dreams to stand out from the crowd and live an extraordinary life.

Stop by our Itty Bitty™ website to find interesting blog entries regarding Pro Cheerleading

www.IttyBittyPublishing.com

Or visit Haley Marie McClain Hill at

haleymcclainhill.com

Table of Contents

Introduction
Secret 1. Bring It On: All or Nothing
Secret 2. Rookies vs. Vets
Secret 3. Way More Than Your Average Side Gig
Secret 4. Hairography + Performance = An Pro Cheer Director's Dream
Secret 5. You Make the Uniform, the Uniform Doesn't Make You
Secret 6. Your Crash Course on the Game of Football
Secret 7. Crush the Interview, Make the Team
Secret 8. How to Secure Your Spot in Your 20-Second Intro
Secret 9. Why "Babes Supporting Babes" Should Be One of Your Core Values
Secret 10. Perfect Practice Makes Perfect
Secret 11. Put Your Game Face On: It's Audition Day!
Secret 12. Behind the Scenes of Your First PRo Cheerleading Practice
Secret 13. Live, Love, Gameday!
Secret 14. Say Yes to the Appearances
Secret 15. Why Life After Poms Is Just the Beginning, and How to Success Stack

Introduction by Jessica Ahner

In the dazzling world of pro cheerleading, putting on the iconic uniform and stepping onto the field is nothing short of a dream come true. As I reflect on my personal journey, I am honored to vouch for the invaluable guidance and mentorship provided by someone who not only shaped my experience but has now encapsulated their wisdom in this guide.

Welcome to *Your Amazing Itty Bitty™ Guide to the Pro Cheerleading World,* a book that transcends the sparkle and glamour, diving into the heart and soul of what it takes to make a pro cheerleading team. My name is Jessica Ahner, and I am not just a cheerleader; I am a living testament to the transformative power of Haley's cheerleading guide.

From the moment you set your mind on auditioning for a pro cheerleading team up to the moment you make the team, this book is composed of insights crafted by my mentor, whose unwavering support and expertise played a pivotal role in my success. As a mentor, Haley possesses a unique ability to inspire and guide aspiring cheerleaders, transforming raw talent into refined performances that captivate audiences on the biggest football stages.

In these pages, you'll discover insider secrets on how to be not only physically, but also mentally prepared to secure a coveted spot on a pro cheerleading squad and thrive in a demanding and competitive environment. Haley shares her wealth of knowledge, from mastering team-specific styles to having a confident pro cheerleader mindset to ensuring that every aspiring cheerleader is equipped with the tools needed to navigate the challenges and embrace the triumphs of this exhilarating journey.

So, whether you're a hopeful candidate seeking a spot on the sidelines, a veteran looking to become a pro-bowl cheerleader, or an enthusiast eager to peek behind the pom poms, join me on this transformative expedition. This is not just a guide; it's a celebration of female empowerment that propels you beyond the sidelines and into the heart of the pro cheerleading experience.

Let the journey begin!

Jessica Ahner – United States Air Force Officer and 2023-2024 Baltimore Ravens NFL Cheerleading Rookie of the Year

Secret 1
Bring It On: All or Nothing

Your dream to be a pro cheerleader has been placed on your heart for a reason. After competing, performing, and coaching in this world, I've noticed the one difference between a good dancer not selected by the judges and the triple-threat dancer who becomes the one the team has to have. That difference is *mindset*.

1. Start by taking an audit of your pro cheerleading mindset. Ask yourself these questions and write down where you are now, then write down where you want to be in the future. How are you? What is your pro cheerleader mindset? Do you feel balanced in your day-to-day life? How do you fuel your mind and body? What is your confidence level? What are your organizational skills? How do you invest in your pro-dance career?
2. Remember that you are what you think. Shift your thoughts away from, "I'm so nervous," and, "There's no way I can compete against all the other dancers," to, "I have the inner drive and passion to make my dreams come true," and, "I'm an asset to any team; why wouldn't they choose me?"

Giving It 100% Effort Is Easier Than 98% Effort

There are two types of people in this world: those who take action today and those who wait around for tomorrow. With less than two percent of college cheerleaders getting an opportunity to make a pro cheerleading team, there's only room for those who fully commit.

- When tryout dates come out, block off your calendar and treat it like any other official event coming up in your life. Gail Mathews, a psychology professor at Dominican University in California, conducted a study on goal-setting with 267 participants. She found that participants were 42% more likely to achieve their goals just by writing them down.
- Next, build a virtual vision board with your dream team clearly featured. Use pictures representing your ideal life and make them the wallpaper on your phone. Neuroscientist Dr. Tara Swart explains, "Looking at images on a vision board primes the brain to grasp opportunities that may otherwise go unnoticed."
- Lastly, let go of people in your life who drain your energy and surround yourself with goal-oriented, energetic, supportive people. Let those stars help you shine.

Step 2
Rookies vs. Vets

In the pro cheerleading world, you have to earn your spot every year. So, whether you're looking to make a team for the first time as a rookie or you're a seasoned veteran and cheered with the same team for three years, your coaches will expect you to be on your A game for tryouts.

1. On average there are 36 spots on a pro cheerleading team comprised of veterans and rookies. Depending on the year, there can be veterans who choose to hang up the poms, which means there are more open spots for rookies.
2. Or there can be a year when most of the veterans choose to stay, which means fewer open spots for new members. However, some veterans might lose their spot to a rookie. Your spot is never guaranteed and even when you're on the team, your coaches are observing how you execute your job throughout the season, which might be a deciding factor during tryouts as well. Your rookie class will always be special but be allies with the veterans, because at the end of the day you will all be teammates.

Professional Athletes Only

The difference between an amateur and a professional cheerleader is not just about the money but also the shift in expectations.

- If you're a rookie, even though you're new you'll still be expected to know and perform your choreography full out for practice and gamedays, show up to every practice on time, and uphold all team standards on fitness, social media, and fan interaction.
- If you're a veteran, you're now held to a higher standard and looked to as a leader on the team. There is little room for mistakes; you could even be responsible for helping organize appearances and team bonding events.
- You will most likely have a director who runs team operations and a choreographer in charge of making sure the dances are gameday ready. Your director and choreographer are responsible for upholding the professional standards and legacy of your team. Respect and honor them, and know their vision for the team. Find ways to be an asset by volunteering for extra fan appearances, taking time to be very clear on team dynamics and rules, respecting their time by asking your captain for assistance with smaller tasks, and always showing up with a "team first" mentality.

Step 3
Way More Than Your Average Side Gig

Triple threat pro cheerleaders learn to balance their careers and passions outside their time as professional dancers.

1. Choose a career that works with your cheerleading schedule. For example, practice can be on Tuesday and Thursday nights from 6-8 p.m. and games usually fall on a Sunday and occasionally on Monday or Thursday nights. Your career outside of cheer should be able to allow you those times off.
2. As soon as you know you're trying out for a team, make sure you know the practice and gameday schedules to clearly communicate the time commitment with your other job. Pro cheer directors and choreographers usually allow one or two missed practices/games, but avoid this as much as possible.
3. Your average pay is about $20/hour, and appearances usually range from $50 to $2,000 per hour. Account for travel and hotels if you don't live close to your practice facility. You will only cheer home games unless your team makes it to the Super Bowl.

Soak In Every Second of Your Season

Being a pro cheerleader is more than showing up for practice and games. To take advantage of this extraordinary experience, make time for the extra opportunities that will be given to you.

- Appearances are the best way for you to get to know your teammates and city. Your director is contacted by organizations around the city for cheerleaders to attend events. You could be invited to a grand opening of a new store, or your pro team could have a season opener event for season ticket holders, or maybe the Super Bowl is in town and you are chosen to do an event on national TV. I highly recommend saying yes to as many appearances as possible because they can be an awesome source of extra income and you will be able to network and build valuable relationships while you're on and off the team.
- Another recommendation is utilizing your status as a pro cheerleader to build your personal brand. If you can post about your experience on social media, acquire brand affiliate partner-ships, or even launch your own pro cheerleading-style dance classes, there are many ways for you to build your reputation and become a better asset to your team.

Step 4
Hairography + Performance = A Pro Cheer Director's Dream

Okay, now that you're more aware of the team dynamics and environment, let's get into the good stuff: your love of dance. Your dance ability is a gift and one of the purest ways of self-love and expression. When you let your light shine, the judges and coaches will have no choice but to stop and pay attention to you.

1. Most women trying out for a pro cheerleading team will have over a decade of dance, cheer, and/or gymnastics experience.
2. It's important to have a strong foundation of hip-hop, jazz, and pom. At a minimum, you want to have a solid double pirouette, strong leaps, above-eye-level high kicks, and the ability to pick up hip-hop and pom choreography. In order to show up and show out, I recommend being able to throw a few dance tricks or even tumble.

When directors and choreographers see a multi-faceted cheerleader, one that can flip or has gorgeous kicks, they can utilize you in different settings and you might even be considered for a solo part in a routine.

Choose Your Favorite Dance Style and Rock It

Judges look for a versatile dancer with great technique and the ability to dance with the team.

- Let me give you an example. To meet the dance requirements for the Atlanta Falcons cheerleaders, you need to be able to pick up their sassy, hip-hop-based choreography. This team might not be for you if you're looking for a team that dances to sportier and rock-and-roll music like the San Francisco 49ers Gold Rush cheerleaders. Choose what feels good for your body!
- Another example is the Dallas Cowboys cheerleaders. Arguably, they're the most technically trained dancers in the league. They focus heavily on performing "Texas big," and also have incredible skills like a triple pirouette into Rockette-level kicks, and hip-hop rhythm to die for.
- The one non-negotiable on every team is your performance value. Even if you're a less-experienced dancer, adding a hair flip and exaggerating a simple motion with a powerful stance and high chin adds a wow factor. You have to imagine fans in the 300 sections being able to see you perform on the field. The bigger the better, but keep it clean.

Step 5
You Make the Uniform, the Uniform Doesn't Make You

You are beautiful inside and out. My job is to showcase every side of you to make you the most compelling candidate for auditions.

1. Audition attire: Prepare two to three audition outfits since tryouts are usually multiple days long. Judges may ask you to wear the same outfit to help them remember you easily, but always have backups just in case. Choose one or two-piece outfits that accentuate your shape, with sparkle accents and colors that flatter you.
2. Fitness: I'll put this bluntly: be in the best shape of your life. You are now a professional athlete, so your health and fitness need to be top priority. Weight training, high-intensity interval training (HIIT), and dance cardio will get you where you need to be for auditions.
3. Hair and makeup: Consult a hairstylist and makeup artist to give you a professional gameday look. Get comfortable dancing with your hair down and sweating in full-face makeup.

Glam Goals and Girl Bosses

When you look good, you feel good. When you feel good, you perform well. When you perform well, you make the team, over, and over again.

- Bring extra everything! Eyelashes, socks, pantyhose, sequins, hair curler, brush, eyeliner. You don't want to be there and forget a key part of your look.
- Research what current girls on the team are sporting for auditions and practice. You can learn a lot about what the coaches look for by observing the current team. Go on social media to see if the team wants more natural glam, or if they like big hair.
- Fuel your body from the inside out. Consult a nutritionist or personal trainer to make sure your body has the energy it needs for audition days. They can last six to eight hours; you could be dancing over 50% of the time. The best way to prepare is months of advance rigorous weight and dance training. Judges look for a strong dancer.
- Make sure your audition attire is durable. You need to jump, dance, and kick without worrying something might rip or break. You want to be a bold, confident dancer. Your outfit will be one of the first reference points that show the coaches your personality.

Step 6
Your Crash Course on the Game of Football

Trust me, if you know these basic pro football fun facts, not only will you enjoy cheering for the game because you will know what's going on, but you will also impress your football-fanatic friends and earn brownie points.

1. There are 32 pro football teams. They are divided into two conferences: the American Football Conference (AFC) and the National Football Conference (NFC). There are four divisions within those conferences. Each conference has an east, west, north, and south division. Make sure you know which division your team is in.
2. Starting in the 2021 season, there will be 18 weeks of pro football games in a season: 17 games and one bye week, which is a rest week.
3. When it comes to positions, the most popular ones you'll hear most often on offense are quarterback, wide receiver, running back, and on defense are linebacker, corner, and safety. For each team on the field, there are 11 players at a time on offense and defense.

Did You Know?

Believe it or not, pro football has the largest TV audience in the world and is expanding more and more. Talking football is a perfect conversation starter, whether you're on a team or not. Football connects you with people around the world! Steal these fun football facts to spice up your daily interactions:

- Pro Football players weren't required to wear helmets until 1943.
- The Chicago Bears had six tie games in 1932.
- A 30-second commercial in the 2021 Super Bowl cost over $5 million.
- More than 100 million people typically watch the Super Bowl every year, and they eat roughly 14,500 tons of chips!
- The Dallas Cowboys team is worth over $5 billion, one of the most valuable franchises in all of sports.

Make sure you know the following about the pro team you want to try out for: most famous current and previous players, head coach, defensive/offensive coordinator, how many Super Bowls they've won, team mascot, stadium name, team owner, team colors, last year's record, draft players just picked up, and how many people fit in the stadium.

I also recommend downloading the Football is Sexy app for more football facts.

Step 7
Crush the Interview, Make the Team

When you make the team, you will be an ambassador for a multi-million-dollar organization. Your interview portion of the audition process shows your director exactly how you will speak and present yourself to fans, executives, and even media outlets.

1. Prepare for questions like: What was your biggest challenge and how did you overcome it? What are you most passionate about? What's the last book you read and what you learned from it? What do you expect to get from being on this team? What's your biggest strength and how will you bring it to the team?
2. Although this is an interview for you, make sure you prepare a few questions to ask the interviewer. For example: What qualities does your highest performing cheerleader exhibit?

Make sure you wear:

1. A mature, business professional outfit that is timeless and classy.
2. Natural hair and makeup that enhances your look (but not full gameday glam).

Non-verbal Communication Is Just as Powerful as Verbal Communication

Although you will receive your interview time and date sometime throughout the audition process, the expectation is that you are being interviewed the entire tryout.

- Before the interview, you will meet aspiring, current, and former cheerleaders and other important people in the organization. Be kind and welcoming to everyone. Be in a competitive mindset and stay focused but greet everyone, be yourself, and keep it light and friendly.
- During your interview make sure your posture is impeccable, have great eye contact, use your hands appropriately and conversationally, bring your resume or notebook just in case and know that even if you don't know the answers to all the questions, you can always spin them to your advantage by showing your personality and sharing something you know.
- After your interview, shake hands and make sure you smile! Bonus: bring a thank-you card with the interviewer's name, and a thoughtful message. This is one thing most people don't do. It will definitely set you apart from the crowd.

Step 8
How to Secure Your Spot in Your 20-Second Intro

There's a moment in each interview when the judges ask each contestant to introduce herself.

1. It should be quick, fun, and intriguing. You want to come across as confident, well-rounded, down-to-earth, and excited to audition.
2. Here's an example of mine: "Hi judges! I'm Haley McClain Hill. I'm 28 years old, originally from Stroudsburg, PA. I just graduated from Penn State with a degree in math. I'm currently an officer in the United States Air Force. I just launched my first business, TORCH, and my goal is to empower military women around the world with fashionable and tactical uniforms. Thank you!"
3. Before you write your intro, pick the most interesting things you want them to know. How will you show them you're an ideal candidate for the team? How do you want them to feel about your intro and meeting you for the first time?

How to Destroy Your Chances of Making the Team in 20 Seconds

Now I want to show you a few things that will immediately lower your chances of making any team. Avoid these at all costs! For rookies trying out for the first time **do not:**

- Show up late
- Talk bad about other girls
- Give up in the middle of the choreography
- Hide in the back and not talk to anyone
- Be unprofessional in any way
- Show up without all audition essentials
- Show up out of shape
- Have a poor-quality headshot

For veterans looking to earn their spot back, **do not:**

- Miss practice without explanation
- Show up to practice without knowing the choreography
- Show up late to appearances
- Have a catty attitude with girls on the team
- Get complacent and assume you're going to make the team
- Post unbecoming content on social media or show poor sportsmanship with fans
- Come to practice/gamedays with a negative attitude

Step 9
Why "Babes Support Babes" Should Be One of Your Core Values

When I cheered with the San Francisco 49ers Gold Rush cheerleaders, my director had a saying she shared with us: "Babes support babes." This became our team mantra and a core value that stuck with me even after I hung up my poms. Let's take a second to put yourself in a pro cheer director's shoes on audition day. She will ask herself questions like the following.

1. Who shows me they'll show up on time, and come to practice prepared with a positive attitude?
2. Which girl brings it 100% and takes correction gracefully?
3. How are this rookie's dance skills compared to a veteran?
4. We have a lot of media coverage coming up this season; who had the best interview? Who can I put in front of a reporter?
5. Who has an awesome career outside the team we can highlight to our fans and inspire the next generation of women?
6. I want these girls to get along and build lifelong friendships. Who is a genuinely good person and team player?

Always Remember You're an Inspiration to Younger Cheerleaders Looking Up to You

The difference between a good and great pro cheerleader is understanding that this gig is bigger than yourself.

- You have an opportunity to inspire the next generation of cheerleaders to be great and set the bar high.
- What do you post on social media? How do you interact with fans at games?
- Live with integrity and uphold the legacy of the amazing women who have come before you and will come after you.
- Your director wants to see the team get better and better.
- Do you invest in yourself, your education, your mental and physical health?
- Do you volunteer your time to invest in your community? How do you give back?
- Do you step outside your comfort zone, take calculated risks, and grow as a woman?
- What lessons have you learned from your experience and do you share that knowledge with others so they can be better dancers too?

Step 10
Perfect Practice Makes Perfect

The way you do anything is the way you do everything. The same goes for mock auditions.

1. Create the most realistic mock audition environment you can. Wear your tryout attire, do your hair and makeup, go to a place with limited distractions, and run through an entire audition.
2. Have friends, family, former pro cheerleaders, or pro cheerleading prep programs be judges. Have them write honest feedback on your performance, interview, and overall pro cheerleader aesthetic.
3. Don't forget to practice your 20-second intro before performing your choreography. When you perform, it should be full out! If you can, have someone quickly choreograph an extra eight counts on the spot to test your ability to quickly pick up choreography. That's a bonus to prep you for unexpected changes that might come up at auditions.
4. Don't interrupt the mock audition at any time. Go from beginning to end to see what it feels like to keep going even if you mess up. Learn to adapt and move forward.

Lessons From a Real-Life Mock Pro Cheerleader Audition

You may use this successful mock audition template for when you are ready:

- Wear your audition outfit and also do your hair and makeup exactly like you will in auditions. You want to know how everything feels when you are performing full out.
- Start your mock audition with a 20-second intro. Make it strong but not too long. Choose a clear and more succinct intro that gives the judges a quick glimpse of who you are and how well you present yourself.
- In your dance portion, focus on keeping your chin and chest high. It's okay to make occasional eye contact with the judges but you want to showcase your ability to project your motions to the stadium's nosebleed section. Even if you mess up, keep smiling and dancing.
- Immediately transition into your interview portion. Change into your interview outfit and make sure your mock audition facilitator asks you a mix of personal and pro football knowledge questions. Stay calm, honest, and authentic even if you do not have all the right answers.
- Remember to be open to feedback when you have finished.

Step 11
Put Your Game Face On: It's Audition Day!

To round out your expectations and understanding of tryouts, here's a sample itinerary of what your audition days will look like:

1. Show up to the stadium to receive your audition number! There will be hundreds of girls there, so stay focused, but also try to make connections.
2. Make sure you bring your resume, audition application, all audition attire, water, snacks, phone charger, change of cozy clothes, a blanket just in case you can relax in a corner while waiting to perform, and headphones to practice the choreography.
3. Warm up as a group, learn the choreography, and then break into small groups to perform.
4. Typically, there is a first round of cuts after this.
5. When you make it through to the next round, you will learn more choreography, and then be assigned an interview date and time.
6. You will perform again, have your interview, and then one more final round.

Making Your Dream Team

When you become a rookie finalist, your team director and choreographer will want to see you dance with the veterans.

- Finals are a time when everyone feels a little tired.
- You've danced for hours multiple days in a row, and now the judges want to see if you have what it takes to perform under pressure.
- They will match you with veterans to see how you mesh with the team.
- Veterans at this point have to show they haven't become complacent and they want their spot just as much as the incoming rookie.
- After you dance, the judges deliberate. This could take a couple hours or it could take months. You will usually know in May or June, because the newly selected team has to begin practice for the upcoming pro season.
- When the team is announced, and you see your name—celebrate! You did it! You've beaten the odds and should be incredibly proud of yourself.
- Work begins very quickly after the team is announced. Look for emails, connect with veterans, and meet your rookie class. It's time to find out your practice schedule and start learning all the new choreography for the season.

Secret 12
Behind the Scenes of Your First Pro Cheerleading Practice

This is the moment you have been waiting for, your first practice. You are officially a pro!

1. Make sure you arrive 15 minutes early with your hair and makeup done.
2. Make friends with a teammate as soon as you can so you can remind each other of everything you might need to bring to practice, i.e., you usually have a team outfit for practice, so make sure you're wearing the right set. Also, you might have to fill out contracts, know the choreography, or bring in documents so you get paid. Help each other out!
3. You will all warm up together and begin learning sideline routines usually carried over from previous seasons. You will find out how gameday is structured, basic guidelines for appearances, and participate in team bonding activities. This first practice lays the groundwork for the entire season.
4. Be a sponge! Take notes. Ask questions. Listen more than you speak. This is the time to make mistakes and to learn how to not repeat them.

You Need Fuel for Your Body and Passion in Your Heart

When I cheered on the Atlanta Falcons, we practiced for three hours on Tuesdays and Thursdays. When I cheered with the 49ers, I had a six-hour practice every Saturday. If you don't prioritize your health and fitness, you won't be a strong asset to your team.

- Make sure you eat a lot of protein and stay hydrated.
- Sleep six to eight hours the night before practice.
- Connect with teammates to practice new choreography to be ready to perform for your coaches.
- Schedule transportation well in advance and make sure to communicate if you might be late or unable to make it.
- Prioritize strengthening your muscles throughout the season to get stronger, which makes practice easier.

You can't expect to crush practice every week if you're only putting in time during set hours. Know this requires you to do extra work at home to truly be considered a triple threat on the team.

- Take extra dance classes.
- Attend voluntary team bonding events.
- Show that you love what you do.

Secret 13
Live, Love, Gameday!

Your first preseason game will always be one of the most special days of your pro cheerleading career. I still remember the first time I stepped out onto the Mercedes Benz field. Let's walk through a typical pre-gameday schedule:

1. If you have a game that starts at noon you will most likely need to arrive by eight a.m. You will have a parking pass or carpool with your teammates and head directly to your team locker room.
2. Everyone will be required to show up with minimal hair and makeup, but once in the locker room, everyone will get in full glam, listening to music, stretching, and getting into practice gear.
3. You will warm up together, then head out for a field rehearsal. This is where you mark your routines exactly where you will perform them for the game. Come prepared, know your choreography, and listen for directions.
4. You will head back to the locker room to change into your gameday uniform and a select group will head out for pre-game appearances.

The Excitement, the Nerves, and the Stardom

Make sure you practice everything you need during pregame, because the next time you perform, it will be on the field in front of the fans!

- You normally perform three times during a game: before kickoff, between the first and second quarters, and between the third and fourth quarters. If there's a special performance, you might cheer during halftime, but most of the time that's when you go back to the locker room, touch up hair and makeup, and grab something to eat.
- During the entire game, you'll be standing in one of the corners with your "line." Your line consists of rookies, veterans, and a captain. Your captain will lead you through sideline dances and chants when the team is on offense and defense. Make sure you smile, cheer, and dance the entire time! Always look to your captain for direction. Watch for incoming football players or balls; you don't want to get tackled accidentally!
- Whether we win or lose, your job is to be the star of the show! Never engage with disgruntled fans.
- After the game, you rally with your coach and then safely leave the stadium.

Secret 14
Say Yes to the Appearances

The secret to capitalizing on your pro cheerleading experience is not only attending games and practices, but also scheduling bookings for as many appearances as possible.

1. There are gameday appearances and there are appearances during the week. Your director will reach out and ask the team if anyone is available to attend an event requesting cheerleaders. There's a per-hour rate and a time commitment.
2. You will be responsible for traveling there, arriving on time, and interacting with attendees. You will usually go with one or two teammates, as well as a security guard for safety.
3. You are a reflection of your entire team during appearances. Make sure you're presentable, friendly, and professional. Be prepared for a lot of pictures. The more you engage in conversation and questions by truly being present at the event, the more fun you'll have. You might have an opportunity to dance, so be sure you know your choreography, which could change if you perform in a smaller group.

Why Are Pro Cheerleaders So Good at Networking?

The skill of networking is perfectly aligned with cheer because you've been trained to build genuine connections and encourage others.

- When you attend these appearances, you don't know who you might meet.
- There could be a parent who wants you to help train their daughter to be a better dancer, or a CEO hiring new staff.
- There are even international opportunities to do awesome things like cheer in a Chinese New Year parade in Hong Kong, or visit a military base on a USO tour.

My favorite part about being a pro cheerleader was all the amazing people I met and stayed connected with. Here are a few pointers on how to build and maintain connections:

- When you initially meet fans or other people at events, always ask their names and do your best to remember them.
- Ask questions about their life, maintain eye contact, and smile to make them feel seen and heard.
- Build your own LinkedIn profile and keep it updated so other professionals you meet can find you and keep up with your success.

Secret 15
Why Life After Poms Is Just the Beginning, and How to Success Stack

Congratulations! Imagine you've cheered on your dream team for two-plus years and you're ready to move on to the next adventure. Now what?

1. Take a minute to reflect on your experiences, gamedays, appearances, team bonding events, and ask yourself if you're ready to move on.
2. Start thinking about the next move. It's better to be thinking about life after poms while you're still cheering to ensure a smooth transition.
3. You want to start success stacking which means you study your past successes, collect all the connections you have built, and use that past experience to build a path to your next big success.

You have an infinite number of options for success after you retire from cheer.

1. You now have an incredible personal brand. You can write a book, share your story, become a motivational speaker, or build your own business.
2. You can teach and give back to the dance community.

Once a Cheerleader, Always a Cheerleader

You are forever part of the pro cheerleading family. It is more powerful than you think. You have learned the following:

- How to be resilient
- How to be an asset to a team
- How to show up with a positive attitude in every situation
- How to motivate people
- How to practice hard until you do it right
- How to bounce back from obstacles
- How to have the inner drive to strive for excellence

I am so proud of you! Taking risks and dreaming big is better than having regrets. You have conquered one of the most sought-after positions in the world, so don't stop now. The sky is the limit. Continue challenging yourself and pushing your limits.

Stay positive and be a light to everyone you come across in life, just like you did on the field. Take this new mindset and the experiences you've had in the pro cheerleading world and become a champion in other areas of life you're passionate about. Use this success and victory as motivation for greater ambition.

You've finished. Before you go...

Post/Share that you finished this book.

Please star rate this book.

Reviews are solid gold to writers. Please take a few minutes to give us some itty bitty feedback.

ABOUT THE AUTHOR

Haley Marie McClain Hill has always made sure her life is full of love and creativity. She is an award-winning entrepreneur, two-time former NFL cheerleader, and United States Air Force veteran.

Her two companies, TORCH Warriorwear and Seek and Set Free, come from the two worlds that have given her so much: the military and the NFL cheerleading world. Her brands have uplifted thousands of women around the globe, lighting the torch for amazing women to do more amazing things.

She won the 2022 Veteran Shark Tank Pitch competition where she received a $50,000 grant which kicked off her success in the business world. She is now the 2023 Founders Live Minnesota Pitch Competition winner and was also seen getting a deal on ABC's Shark Tank Season 15. She loves attending military, entrepreneurship, and athlete-focused conferences where she can speak and listen to women with big dreams.

She has cheered over 100 NFL and collegiate football games and gives back to cheer and dance spaces by offering workshops at academies and pro-cheerleading team retreats.

Haley has advised startup fashion brand companies, led over 300+ airmen while a first lieutenant in the US Air Force, and has appeared on the game show *Beat Shazaam!*

Haley believes in being multi-passionate and leading with love. She fearlessly seeks what sets her soul on fire. She believes her purpose is to inspire others to live their dream lives! She is always ready to help you start a business, win that pitch competition, move up in your career, make that team, and ultimately become the best version of you!

If you enjoyed this Itty Bitty™ book you might also like …

- **Your Amazing Itty Bitty™ Fear Busting Book by Lucetta Zaytoun**

- **Your Amazing Itty Bitty™ Affirmations Book by Micaela Passeri**

- **Your Amazing Itty Bitty™ Purpose Book by Gretchen Downey**

- **Your Amazing Itty Bitty™ Book on the Power of Positive Playlists by John Ivor Chester, III**

or any of the many Amazing Itty Bitty™ books available online at
www.ittybittypublishing.com

www.ingramcontent.com/pod-product-compliance
Lightning Source LLC
Chambersburg PA
CBHW061306040426
42444CB00010B/2536